The MANIFESTOR'S PLAYBOOK

How to Manifest Your Dream Life Using the Law of Attraction

An Interactive Playbook by

Steve L Chong

THE MANIFESTOR'S PLAYBOOK:

How to Manifest Your Dream Life

Using the Law of Attraction

ISBN-13: 978-0-9858523-0-6

Ebook: 978-0-9858523-1-3

Library of Congress Number: 2018910107

Published by Steve Chong

www.manifestorsplaybook.com

Dedication

To my parents and sister for all the love, patience, and support for without them, this Playbook would not have been possible.

CONTENTS

	Dedication	iii
	INTRODUCTION	1
#1	What Is Manifestation, Exactly?	3
#2	What Does It Mean to Be A Conscious Manifestor?	6
#3	What Is the Key to Manifesting Our Dreams and Desires?	9
#4	What Is the Law of Attraction?	13
#5	What Separates Successful Manifestors From Ordinary People?	15
#6	What Is the Best Way to Enter A State of Abundance?	17
#7	What Are the Top Ways to Get Your Gratitude In Motion?	20
#8	What Is the Secret Gate to Manifestation?	27
#9	Where Did the Law of Attraction Come From?	30
#10	What Are the Top Ways to Reprogram Your Subconscious Mind?	37
#11	What Is the Formula For Manifesting My Dream Life, Right Now?	49
#12	What Are the Top Ways to Increase Your Manifesting Potential?	63
	CONCLUSION: *Real Magic!*	87

[This is a self-initiation into the world of the manifestor.]

INTRODUCTION

Welcome to ***The Manifestor's Playbook!***
In your hands is everything you need to make your dream life a living breathing reality.

One of our ***greatest abilities*** as humans is that we can ***see the invisible, take what is inside our minds***, and then ***materialize our ideas into the outside physical world*** - right before our very eyes! Nowadays, many people talk about "***MANIFESTATION***" and the "***UNIVERSAL LAWS***" - *yet these concepts still prove to be* ***elusive, nebulous and mysterious.***

Now Is the Time to Get Vitally Clear On The Subject of Manifestation!

No doubt that if you are reading this right now, it is your heart's desire to manifest your ultimate dream life. We have lovingly created this Playbook to let ***YOU*** manifest the life of ***YOUR*** dreams with effortless grace.

You know that you did not just ***randomly*** find this Playbook. You ***"attracted"*** it to yourself just like everything else present in your life. This manifestation guide will help you take the steps today that will change your life forever. It contains everything you need to draw the **success, abundance, and joy** you deserve and desire!

Inside you will find simple, yet extremely effective techniques to help manifest your best life and assist you with clearing the past negative subconscious conditionings which keep us from actualizing our goals. You will experience immediate results and resonate at a much higher level of consciousness as a benefit of using this Playbook!

The answers to all the questions you have always been curious about are within, such as:

What Is "MANIFESTATION" Exactly?

What Does It Mean to Be A Conscious Manifestor?

What Is the Key to Manifesting Our Dreams and Desires?

What Is the Law of Attraction?

What Separates Successful Manifestors From Ordinary People?

What Are the Top Ways to Get Your Gratitude In Motion?

What Is the Best Way to Enter A State of Abundance?

What Is the Secret Gate to Manifestation?

Where Did the Law of Attraction Come From?

What Are the Top Ways to Reprogram Your Subconscious Mind?

What Is the Formula For Manifesting My Dream Life, Right Now?

What Are the Top Ways to Increase Your Manifesting Potential?

The knowledge contained in this Playbook is priceless – it will show you a proven path to a successful, happy, and self-determined life in freedom, rather than in bondage. However, it is solely up to ***YOU*** to *demonstrate* these principles in action in order to breathe life into your visions!

Love and Magic,

Steve Chong

Steve Chong - Creator of The Manifestor's Playbook

CHAPTER 1

What Is Manifestation, Exactly?

Manifesting is the art and science of *intentionally* creating reality.
It is all about making one's dreams come true.

Now, when your thoughts and intentions materialize into this physical reality, the so-called ***"real world"*** - that is the phenomenon known as *manifestation*. It is the completely natural practice of creating your heart's desires - at the time desired.

Hence, to have a true understanding of this concept is essential to finding your soul's purpose and to fulfilling your life's greatest aspirations! ***What Else Could Be More Important?***

Manifestation should not be dismissed as just *"wishful thinking"*, as the doubters and unbelievers often do. For manifested results are not just merely daydreams or wishes in the wind, but scientifically verifiable fact. Realize ***right now*** that you have the capability to change your mindset to start creating the very life you truly desire and deserve, through the power of conscious manifestation.

You are manifesting every day in every way!

Stop for a moment and take a good look around you. *Describe What You See. Go ahead, do it.*

Everything you see before you, someone had first imagined; all that you are sensing around you *right now* was once just a thought in the mind of its creator before it became a physical creation which now appears as real-world phenomena to you, the beholder.

As manifestors, we realize that nothing exists in this material world that did not *first* have its genesis in the mind as a pure thought by its creator; ***everything starts as an idea!***

Take for example a chair, table, or spoon. ***How did it get there?*** It did not just appear randomly, *now did it?* Logically, it had to have been invented, designed, and manufactured prior to your experience with the object.

A simple concrete example of a common manifestation that illustrates how we are "*manifesting*" all the time every day, is when we manifest meals to satisfy our own hunger. Think back to your most recent meal. *Can you explain how exactly you manifested your meal? How did it get there? How was it that a meal actually materialized in front of you for consumption? How was it that your specific meal got to appear before you when there was nothing there prior? What were the literal steps involved?*

Before you took your first bite, was there not a *process* involved to receiving your food? Let us break it down:

Prompted by hunger, the process of manifesting your meal was initially sparked by the idea and visualization of the chosen cuisine you wished to eat. Maybe it was pizza or maybe a steak or maybe a vegetarian feast. Once you had a mental picture of your desired meal, only then could you or someone else take the action steps necessary to actually *materialize* the meal and get it ready for consumption.

Then ***voilà!*** What was once just a figment of your imagination has become a tangible reality in front of you, ready to be consumed by its manifestor. Now whether that meant going to the grocery store or restaurant for carry-out, or calling out for delivery, or possibly even preparing the meal yourself from scratch in the kitchen – pragmatic action by the manifestor was necessary to make it real.

That is the raw and simple power of manifestation in everyday action!

And just like in manifesting meals, know that we all have the innate potential to bring any of our desired ideas into fruition and that we can *directly* shape the very universe in which we live and breathe!

CHAPTER 2

What Does It Mean to Be A Conscious Manifestor?

The main concept behind conscious manifestation is that: ***"You Create Your Own Reality."***

You have a power so simple to access and operate; yet, most people are completely unaware of the control and influence they possess! Right now, this very moment you are creating the future. And it is through your ***beliefs*** that this reality is being created.

Everyone has the ability to manifest anything they desire, be it wealth, optimum health, love, compassion, houses, cars, world-travel, vacations, peace of mind, etc. Your mind is so powerful that it creates the reality you experience from the *inside out*. All of us have the power to be the creators of the future, designers of our own destinies.

Within you is tremendous power of transcendental proportions!

You have more control over the world you live in than you could possibly imagine; *for what you believe becomes your reality.* Although it may be difficult to believe at times, but everything you have ever experienced in your life has been your own creation. *We ourselves are the makers of ourselves.*

Contrary to popular belief, your life is not happening to you - ***you are creating it!***

Yes, exactly where you are *right here, right now* is based on the decisions you have made in the past. However, most people are completely oblivious to the powerful capabilities they possess. Whether we consciously choose them or not, you are in a constant state of manifesting and you are producing a new manifestation literally as fast as you can think. *The truth is that we are incredible manifesting machines – continuously creating the present moment all the time through our* ***thoughts, words and deeds****.*

We are literally creating the world around ourselves. Everything we think, everything we feel and everything we do becomes part of the fabric of our environment, the people around us, and the community we live in. That is how powerful we are. *Change your mind and the world changes.*

All of our thoughts, conscious and even more so our ***subconscious***, directly affect how things manifest around and within us. Since most people are not aware of all the manifestations being generated by their mind; they simply do not pay attention to the quality of their thoughts, inner dialogue, or emotional state. They fail to recognize the power of their minds as being the cause of their success or failure.

Awareness is the key and with awareness comes change.

Belief is a construct and just like any other construct - *it can be manipulated and changed.* You can bend and shape it according to the strength of your will.

The reality is that by learning to control your thoughts and emotions you can ***BE, DO, and HAVE*** anything in life! Once you are awakened to this quintessential, yet often obscured fact of life, you all of a sudden become very careful about what you think about, what you say, and what you do. If you are not in control of your thoughts and emotions, it means that you are manifesting through life unconsciously, and worse yet you allow others to create your future for you.

The problem is that the majority of people are not consciously awake to these principles and thus manifest *unconsciously*, creating a conventional reality which constantly confirms and strengthens whatever we have been taught to believe. ***Most people are fast asleep!***

The average person walks around like a zombie, living a boxed life of limitations when in actuality they have the ability to meticulously craft everything in their lives. So, if you do not like any area of your life, take time to reexamine, reflect, and make different choices.

Limitations only exist in the mind and imagination is the key to freedom.

Now in order to manifest a dream, ***one must first have a dream***. Conscious manifestation requires having an active imagination; for manifestation is an inside-out proposition. *What you seek outwardly comes from inside of you.* It must be created in our hearts and minds first. You cannot experience what you cannot conceive.

As conscious beings, we have the *free-will* and ability to create our own thoughts. Although this ability to actively shape reality is something we are all born with, it is deliberately and systematically stymied and stifled by the educational and economic structures that we have grown up within. You are constantly being shielded from this potent self-transformational knowledge by the powers that be.

However, once you acknowledge that it is ***YOU*** that creates reality, all power is back in your hands. *Nothing can exist without you!* You are responsible for everything that happens. ***How do you live your life?***

Take control of your life today!

Ask yourself: ***Am I living life by default or by design?***

Am I living my dream or someone else's?

Am I living my best life possible?

There is nothing and no one else to blame.

CHAPTER 3

What Is the Key to Manifesting Our Dreams and Desires?

It is a simple, yet multidimensional four-step process illustrated by the acronym **I-C-A-N.**

When followed carefully, it will guide you to the achievement of your future visions. This is a great acronym given that *"I CAN"* is one of the potent positive affirmations in existence. Each letter stands for a different phase of the manifestation process:

I: ***Imagination***

C: ***Clarification***

A: ***Activation***

N: ***Nurturation***

First step, *imagine it so* - right now! Yes, based on your passions, visualize your ideal dream being realized in the present moment, as we speak. It is time to answer the question:

What is your Ultimate Big Life Dream?

Let us go into the future and live it out now. Choose what dream of yours to manifest. Creatively visualize, *with great emotional power*, the full realization of your ultimate life dream!

Take a few moments to meditate and let your mind run free. ***Now put yourself in the picture!***

Allow yourself to experience this in a way that engages all of your senses - ***be in the moment!*** *Feel the feelings of your dream fulfilled: see the sights, taste the flavors, smell the aromas, make it as compelling, detailed, and specific as humanly possible!*

Your dream is your gift - it is unique to you!

Secondly, clarify the top goals required to make your big life dream possible. This must be stated in a concrete way using names, numbers, and specific dates. *Know* ***why****, know* ***how****, know* ***when****, know with* ***whom****.* ***See sharply*** exactly what you desire!

Your goals must be made vivid, visceral, and vivacious to increase their efficacy. *If you do not know what you truly want, then how can it ever be manifested?* So be sure your message is clear and focused and ensure each of your goals are measurable along the journey.

Be unapologetic about what you want! Now is not the time to hold back. ***Be brave. Be bold.***

And just like ordering food at a restaurant: if you clearly state your order, the server knows exactly what to bring you. But if your order is confusing and you are not quite exactly sure how you want your food prepared, the chances that your order will come out *not* to your liking dramatically increases.

Show and tell the universe exactly what you what from it. You determine exactly what it is you want to ***BE***, ***DO*** and ***HAVE*** in life. The clearer and more vibrant the mental picture, the faster it manifests!

Thirdly, the most vital step is to take deliberate, inspired, and pragmatic action. All things are possible but without stimulation nothing happens.

Demonstrating inspired action is crucial to making dreams real. *Action releases your intention - it starts the energy moving!* So once you recognize what your dream actually is, take deliberate and pragmatic action as soon as possible.

Taking genuine tangible action steps is a living ***demonstration*** of your commitment to your intentions. Once you demonstrate and exemplify your true beliefs, the Universe has no other choice than to realize those beliefs and desires. ***But the magic cannot happen until you take that first action step!***

So be sure to break down your goals into small, digestible steps and have faith that it will happen the way you intend it to be. This unstoppable combination of creative inspiration and practical action ensures success.

No one is going to come up to you with your dream fully manifested on a Silver Platter. And if someone actually were to do that for you would not be able to appreciate it as it was not earned.

The bottom line is that your dreams will remain ***unmanifest*** without your active participation!

Finally, now that your dream seeds have been securely planted, tend them carefully. They need to be nurtured with your love, energy, absolute attention, and tender care in order for them to grow to fruition. *Because after all, is it not nurturing care that makes everything grow?*

Just like an acorn seed grows into an oak tree from roots to stem, then branches, and leaves, there are natural patterns of growth. Proper goal nurturance will help turn visions into living realities. It is vital to make a conscious effort to nurture your dreams and goals. It is about commitment defined by action, not just words!

If not you, then who?

By applying this **I-C-A-N method**, you can manifest any and all of your heart's desires. This is the formula to manifest anything!

There you have it: ***What is your heart's desire? What were you born to do?***

What will YOU manifest?

Of course, this is only a brief introduction to the creation process. We will go more in depth, where you will get the opportunity to manifest ***YOUR OWN*** ultimate big life dream and the specific goals necessary to make that dream reality, as we progress through this Playbook together.

CHAPTER 4

What Is the Law of Attraction?

The Law of Attraction simply states that ***LIKE attracts LIKE***.

Positive energy attracts positive energy and negative energy attracts negative energy.

Isaac Newton's third law of motion states every action has an equal and opposite reaction. Similarly, each ***thought*** you think, each ***emotion*** you feel, and each ***action*** you take creates an energy vibration, a ***resonance*** that can either push or pull.

Everything is energy vibrating at its own frequency!

The Law of Attraction is invariably working all the time, meaning that akin to a ***MAGNET*** - you will draw to yourself the things, people, and experiences that resonate to the vibrational frequency you are presently broadcasting.

Conversely, you will repel those things, people, and experiences that are not on the same resonance.

Your belief is very powerful whether it is true or not. And the Law of Attraction will dependably work, whether you understand it or not. In truth, what we attract or repel depends on the frequencies we are broadcasting through our **emotional state**.

Whatever frequency you match, that is the reality you get in return. If you match the frequency of wealth, prosperity, abundance, and success - you have **no choice** but to attract more of that energy into your life. But if you believe that you are limited in your capacity to grow in your life, career, relationships, or financial standing – then this belief will be dutifully realized.

Because everything you create originates in the mind, the *quality* of the thoughts and feelings that surround your dreams and goals determines your likelihood of achieving them. High vibrational emotions such as joy, love, forgiveness, compassion, gratitude, patience, and peace raise your vibration while emotions rooted in negativity such as fear, doubt, worry, anger, greed, attachment, jealousy, and resentment are all at the bottom of the energy spectrum lowering your state of resonance.

Those who choose to concentrate on lack, scarcity, and neediness will find themselves in circumstances that deny them of what little they do have. That is why negative people, negative environments, and negative emotions unfortunately have the ability to block, cripple, or even cancel out your manifestations.

Therefore, it is *imperative* to eliminate negative thinking through practices such as *meditation, exercise, yoga and prayer*!

When you are intently focused on your dreams and your vibration is strong, manifestation is inevitable.

It must happen!

CHAPTER 5

What Separates Successful Manifestors From Ordinary People?

It all comes down to mindset; your ***frame of mind.***

Conscious manifestation success requires being in the right mental state. By operating from an abundance mindset instead of a scarcity mindset, a profound separation occurs between manifestors and the masses of ordinary people.

Abundance means completely believing in yourself, believing that there are more than enough resources for everyone, and that there is plentitude for the future. The abundance mindset says you possess an ***infinite, creative, wealthy mind*** where the only limit to reality is your imagination and the strength of your will. Armed with an abundance mentality, you are unshackling from false limiting self-beliefs that haunt most people; instead you are embracing all the possibilities!

Consequently, the main difference between manifestors from the deluded, distracted masses comes down to their mentality and the successful manifestor's frame of mind is one of ***prosperity and abundance - a true wealth consciousness!***

Standing in staunch opposition to the prosperity mindset is the scarcity mindset and its subsequent poverty-level consciousness. The scarcity mindset says that: *you are not enough, that there are not enough resources for everyone to go around, and that there is not enough for the future*. This toxic, fear-based outlook is represented by a ***finite, competitive mind*** where there is only so much of the pie, a false belief where in order for me to get a larger piece, you must get a smaller piece.

The consequences of operating from a scarcity mentality can be quite painful and debilitating for the individual - creating a life of unnecessary fear, anxiety, desperation, and overall insecurity. An individual trapped in a scarcity mindset will spend most of their waking life fearful, anxious, and generally worrying about the future. They have a difficult time believing in themselves and have been brainwashed by society into constantly behaving from a position of lack.

Often times, people shackled under a scarcity mindset will *self-sabotage* themselves then manufacture endless excuses while looking for others to blame for their misfortunes!

Remember, according to the Law of Attraction, if you believe you must struggle for abundance, you will find yourself in situations that are conducive to struggling. *So in order for you to get the most out of life, you need to get rid of self-limiting beliefs and understand there is no scarcity of opportunity and resources in this Universe!*

Now ask yourself: ***Do you live in constant fear or do you have faith that you can achieve anything?*** Be honest.

Is my focus on abundance or scarcity?

This is not a trick question - it can only be one or the other.

CHAPTER 6

What Is the Best Way to Enter A State of Abundance?

In a word, **gratitude**.

Being authentically grateful is the easiest way to go from negative to positive, and best way to get into an abundance mindset *immediately*, is through the emotion of gratitude - for ***gratitude creates abundance.*** There are two basic approaches to life: Gratitude or Resentment. You choose what role to play.

All the world's a stage. And all the men and women merely players. – William Shakespeare

If you have not noticed already, most successful people in life have great positive attitudes. It is gratefulness that shifts our energy to what is good and that attracts even more of what you want.

Attitude is everything!

When applying the Law of Attraction in your life, do not get too caught up in making endless lists and vision boards and forget one of the most vital components in dream manifesting – **gratitude**, for every thought, idea, and experience has an indelible effect in our brains.

What you do has a ripple effect - to all and everything!

It is very easy to forget how much we have and how lucky we truly are. As our modern materialistic society is deluded by and stuck in endless cycles of consumerism and the dark morose of greed, it is of vital importance to practice an attitude of gratitude. The key is to feel as much gratitude as possible, as deep as you can, as often as you can - because actualizing gratitude sets you into the flow of nature, the Universe.

People, places and things, no matter how big or how small, love them all!

What really changes our perception of our own reality is the practice of gratitude. It makes you happier and you can dramatically increase the amount of pure joy, energy, and feelings of prosperity while decreasing feelings of greed, bitterness, and resentment. Practice replacing doubt, fear, and worry with feelings of abundance because what you are feeling right now is what you are going to attract.

The moment you feel abundant is the moment you start generating wealth. Remember, what you give is what you receive. If you give out gratitude for what you have, you will receive more things to be grateful for. That includes your dreams and your deepest desires. Needless to say, gratitude is a key ingredient to success in all areas of your life.

When you practice and feel gratitude, you are elevating yourself into a higher vibrational state – it is a sheer magical feeling!

Special note: Applying gratitude in your life will produce immediate dividends as gratefulness raises your vibration and of those around you. In fact, *everything is created by you, indeed you are the creator of it all, and you have the conscious will power to change everything you have created!*

What are 10 (or more) things you are grateful for RIGHT NOW?

I am grateful for: ______________________________

I am grateful for: ______________________________

I am grateful for: ______________________________

I am grateful for: ______________________________

I am grateful for: ______________________________

I am grateful for: ______________________________

I am grateful for: ______________________________

I am grateful for: ______________________________

I am grateful for: ______________________________

I am grateful for: ______________________________

I am grateful for: ______________________________

I am grateful for: ______________________________

I am grateful for: ______________________________

I am grateful for: ______________________________

CHAPTER 7

What Are the Top Ways to Get Your Gratitude In Motion?

Gratitude works best when it is... ***in motion.***

Here are seven simple ways to demonstrate thankfulness which brings abundance into your life in return:

#1 Perform Random Acts Of Kindness

Make someone *else* happy. Instead of focusing on your own happiness, focus on someone else for a change. It will make the world a better place.

Being kind to others is also good for your health. By helping others and having a mindset of *charitable giving* increases our own well-being and augments our ability to have even more gratitude.

Helping others helps you!

One way to cultivate more gratitude within yourself is by doing kind, compassionate, and helpful things for others without an expectation of compensation. Start paying things forward and do something good for someone else. Through your generosity, you can potentially affect another's life in a positive way and bring joy to yourself. Just by performing a simple act of kindness, you can trigger a gratitude chain reaction in motion!

How many random acts of kindness can you do today?

No man is an island and the easiest way to remember this is by helping others, whether it is formally through volunteering or informally like helping someone you encounter on the street. Remember, life is a group effort and none of us can do it all on our own.

Success is best when shared. Do something for someone and feel how great it feels afterwards.

#2 Be More Mindful

Be here now.

We all have the natural ability to be present. But too many people nowadays are either so worried about the uncertainties of future occurrences or so caught up dwelling on emotions influenced by negative past experiences, that they miss the brilliance of the *present moment.* This lack of attention can lead to a ton of undesired effects such as stress, bad moods, conflicts, a lack of focus and a sense of disconnectedness.

Just let it be.

Practicing mindfulness is about clearing your mind and purposefully focusing all of your attention on what we are doing in the current moment and accepting it - *without judgement.* This means to fully experience every single moment and savoring what life brings on your way. It is about total sensory engagement in every part of an activity.

You can bring mindfulness to anything you do and find yourself less stressed and more grounded in the process. Any activity such as walking, listening to music, gardening, knitting, or meditating can be a mindful activity as long as it engages your senses and brings your mind back to the present. There are a plentitude of meditation methods and techniques that can help you cultivate and incorporate mindfulness every day. Just choose your favorite activities.

Whatever you do, do it consciously, not mechanically!

In a world full of chaos, mindfulness is the skill needed to create order. When done correctly, you can reduce stress, anxiety, and negative emotions while improving memory, performance, and concentration skills.

How much of your day is spent being in the actual moment, rather than reflecting on the past or planning for the future?

With mindfulness exercises we can harness the ability to root the mind in the present moment and deal with life's challenges in a calm, clear-minded, assertive way. Remember, the more you practice, the more you will reap the benefits without the worries and concerns that most people have.

#3 Say Please and Thank You Often

These 3 words can go a long way.

We have the ability to make a world a better place - simply by being polite and by being mindful of the words we speak. ***Words are everything.*** Words have the power to heal and also the power to destroy.

So always treat others the way you wish to be treated for it is the little decisions in life that make the big difference. When we say *"Please"*, it shows respect and consideration for another's thoughts and feelings. It also empowers them to respond to your request or not.

When we say, *"Thank You"*, it also shows respect and shows appreciation for what another individual has done for you. Just a few words of recognition can help brighten someone's day and it lets them know that their words or deeds did not go unnoticed. *It demonstrates to people that you value them.*

A simple *"Thank You"* can trigger good feelings for everyone involved. Furthermore, it discourages taking people and things for granted and motivates us to provide more help in the future. Gratitude is an extraordinarily positive transformative emotion, and one of the best ways to feel it working in your life is to speak words of thanksgiving to yourself and others.

Write thank you notes and cards whenever possible. A quick email, a simple sticky note, or shout out on social media is enough to let that special person know that you are grateful for having them in your life. It is a great way to increase your own happiness by sharing your gratitude and appreciation.

Being a kind and courteous person can turn somebody's entire day around. Make sure "Please" and "Thank You" are an integral part of your everyday vocabulary. Never forget that none of us have gotten to where we are at today without the help of others.

#4 Listen Intently

Listening is more than just hearing the noises coming out of people's mouths.

Active listening is a skill that is often overlooked in today's self-centered society. An easy way to make somebody feel appreciated and validated is to simply hear them out. *Listening shows that you care.* When you stop worrying about what you are going to say next and instead you listen actively and intentionally, it shows respect and appreciation.

Unfortunately, most of us never *genuinely* listen to people when they are speaking to us. Becoming a good active listener takes patience and practice. Take the time to listen.

You might be surprised by what you hear!

So next time you are in a conversation, make it your intention to fully listen to what the other person is saying to you, without getting lost in your own thoughts. Ask thoughtful questions, do not interrupt – let them have their say. If you do not understand something being communicated, say something instead of playing along. Give constructive feedback and summarize what you heard to show you understand.

Inattention is an insult.

#5 Forgive Others, Forgive Yourself

Forgiveness often does not come easily. Many people carry with them wounds that cause feelings of bitterness, rage, and vengeful thoughts. But if we hold onto these negative emotions, they begin to take a toll on our *own* physical, mental, emotional, and spiritual well-being. Whenever you fail to forgive, you really just end up harming yourself, not the one who hurt you.

Shift your mindset away from playing the role of the victim!

By genuinely forgiving yourself and others, you can now release all the pain, blame, and emotional baggage hindering you and weighing down your subconscious mind. The act of forgiveness breaks the cycle of negative energy that has been holding you back from fulfilling relationships, careers, and lives.

Holding on to anger is like grasping a hot coal with the intent of throwing it at someone else; you are the one who gets burned. – Buddhist Quote

True forgiveness is a voluntary process. One must decide to consciously let go of the anger and resentment they hold as a result of someone else's words or actions. Deciding to forgive is a direct path towards reconciliation and a way of creating peace both in your outer and inner life.

Now reflect on your own shortcomings, lapses in judgement, and other instances in which you needed forgiveness from someone else. Doing this simple exercise will help you empathize with someone who may need your forgiveness.

Is there someone you need to forgive?

Self-forgiveness is also a critical element to your well-being. Because we all know that *"to err is human, to forgive divine"* and that we all make mistakes. By having the courage to face what we have done in the past and acknowledging our mistakes, we can move on with our lives.

When you forgive yourself, you are *transcending* your anger at yourself with love and compassion - the same positive emotions you are giving others.

Can you find the compassion to forgive others and forgive yourself today?

Remember: unforgiveness of any kind leads to the festering of negative energy and the suppression of one's overall spiritual growth.

#6 Stop Complaining

Life is what you make it and one way to creating a more positive life is by eliminating negative and useless statements.

Habitual, chronic complaining affects its victims mentally, emotionally, and physically in profound ways. Complaining is draining - it is a negative behavior that adversely affects our happiness, attitude, and ability to perform. *Beware as this type of childish behavior saps your energy and the energy of those around you!*

Did you know that the act of complaining concentrates your attention on what it identifies as a problem causing more of it to manifest? ***Every time you complain, you are reinforcing a negative state of mind!*** So next time you are tempted or frustrated, instead of just reacting with a bunch of sighs of self-pity and complaints, take a few deep breaths and focus on the positive. Reframe the picture.

How long can you abstain from complaining?

Change comes with awareness. Have you ever tracked how often you complain throughout your day?

Abstain from complaining for 24 hours and realize you can make the shift!

#7 Start A Gratitude Journal
Large and small start collecting all of your grateful moments.

You can begin by creating lists of all the things you are grateful for. A gratitude journal can be a notebook or any piece of paper where you write down things you are grateful for that day. Take a few moments to write it all down. This healthy habit will help you see your life through the lens of abundance, and not lack.

Any time is a good time to make entries to your gratitude journal, you can write as much or as little as you like. The physical act of writing has known therapeutic effects and showing gratitude on a regular basis can raise your awareness of things to be grateful for. The important thing is to establish a daily practice of reminding yourself of all the blessings, gifts, grace, and other good things in your life.

Doing this every day will change your brain!

When you express genuine thanksgiving from your heart, you are radically altering the neural pathways in your brain. Take a minute to read from your journal every night before you go sleep, as focusing on gratitude significantly improves your sense of well-being and life satisfaction.

CHAPTER 8

What Is the Secret Gate to Manifestation?

The secret is that ***reality*** is based on the ***subconscious mind.***

It is not your conscious mind that creates your reality, but it is through your subconscious beliefs - for what we believe ***subconsciously*** is what we make true. *Herein lies the secret of secrets.*

Now, though it is possible to reprogram someone at any age, the framework and contents of one's subconscious mind are basically set in place at an early age, possibly even before puberty. So whatever big or tiny decisions we take as adults, it is largely our subconscious minds and subsequent mental programming and life-scripts that runs the show. That is why our parents, our peers, early experiences, and environment are magnificently influential and immensely pivotal in determining who we ultimately become.

Did you know that the subconscious mind is ***unfathomably*** more powerful than your conscious mind?

The subconscious mind produces what it thinks is real and is fully responsible for creating your reality. And what you plant in your subconscious becomes reality through our ***imaginations.***

Conscious creators are well aware of the role of the subconscious mind, and therefore act accordingly in every circumstance.

You truly are what you think!

Thus, it is by tapping into the power of the subconscious mind that the secret gate to manifesting is **opened!**

The fact of the matter is that vast majority of human cognition occurs in the subconscious mind. This is the thinking that takes place below your conscious awareness. The classic metaphor for this is the iceberg where approximately 80-90% of the mass lies hidden below the water. The submerged portion of the iceberg represents your subconscious mind and the 10-20% above water, the tip of the iceberg represents your conscious *"thinking"* mind. Symbolically, this means 80-90% of our actions and results are determined by our subconscious minds.

What is also supremely interesting about our subconscious minds is that it cannot distinguish between what's ***"real"*** and what is ***"imagined"***. The subconscious mind will actually accept all the thoughts and images that you often repeat or are presented to you without judgement.

All of that information you have ever gathered all gets stored in the subconscious mind. Included are your self-beliefs, your self-image, your self-esteem, and what you believe is possible for you - it is all a bundle of energy that vibrates deep within you. And herein lies the opportunity for you to break the default life-script handed to you and fulfill all ***YOUR*** heart's desires by harnessing the *power of the subconscious mind.*

Since our perception of reality is determined by our beliefs, now you know that you can directly shape the future by *reprogramming* your subconscious mind!

Have you tried to change things in your life but did not get the results that you wanted?

Then your subconscious mind is possibly getting in the way. Remember, whatsoever the subconscious mind *believes* to be true - it immediately makes true. If you say "I am poor" for instance, that is what your subconscious mind believes and will manifest for you.

Whether you think you can or cannot - you will always be correct!

Your entire life experience is being ***fabricated*** by what you ***believe about yourself***. If you believe something is difficult, your subconscious mind will conspire to make it so. If you believe everything is easy, your subconscious mind will show you that as well. So be unmistakably cognizant of what you feed your subconscious! Are you feeding it joy and inspiration or are you feeding it doom-and-gloom?

Everything ultimately becomes a self-fulfilling prophecy!

The world is a reflection of you - what do you want it to look like?

Happy? In bliss? Limitless, full of love and abundance? Healthy, sustainable, and balanced?

***YOU* choose what it looks like. Yes, *YOU*!**

CHAPTER 9

Where Did the Law of Attraction Come From?

The Law of Attraction is actually an amalgamation based on the seven Universal Laws attributed to the ancient author, Hermes Trismegistus. These are the cosmic principles by which everything is governed (no less), and we need to understand them if we want to live in the flow of nature - harmoniously and abundantly.

Positive affirmations, creative visualization, prayer, meditation, and all other manifestation techniques are for nothing if you are not in alignment with the Universal Laws.

The following seven heavenly principles that explain the nature of reality are quoted from a book describing the wisdom taught by Hermes. Written in 1912, by the Three Initiates, *"The Kybalion: Hermetic Philosophy"* is widely considered to be one of the greatest classic and historical texts of all time.

Once you align yourself with the Seven Universal Laws - YOU will experience a complete metamorphosis in every area of your life!

#1 Law of Mentalism

"The all is mind; the universe is mental."

This first law explains that "the all" is spirit, not matter. All creation is possible and has its being from this infinite, intelligent energy and we are all part of this universal living mind.

You see, everything we experience in our physical realm has its origin in the mental realm, the unseen invisible world. Our very existence and reality are merely manifestations of our individual and collective minds.

Everything is formed through thought. Thoughts are creative; they are the means of *CREATION*. Thoughts *are*.... and *become* things. *So be aware of your thoughts as they can create and destroy! Be conscious of your responsibility!*

In the beginning was the Word.... – John 1:1

Everything begins with the perspective of the mind; the world that you see in front of you is all electrical signals being received and perceived by the brain. *Everything you see outside is actually all inside of your mind.* Let me explain, as humans we interpret the external world directly through our 5 material senses: sight, touch, smell, hearing and taste. And it is this sensory nervous system that takes external stimuli and relays them as electrical signals to our brain - forming our inner personal reality - our *consciousness.*

Your brain is telling your eyes what it is seeing. This is happening right now as you are reading these words.

So there it is - everything you see is really just a figment of your imagination.

There is no reality, only perception.

It is all happening in your mind!

#2 Law of Correspondence

"As above, so below; as below so above".

This Hermetic Principle states that the macrocosm is found in the microcosm and vice versa. *All is one.*

Your inner reality creates your outer world. Even more, the outer world is your mirror, when you change, everything around you will change. The external world is an exact reflection of what you think. The predominant thoughts and images we hold in our subconsciousness will begin to manifest themselves in our external circumstances because we manifest by ***being*** who we are. Not be what we are doing.

Manifestation is an inside-out proposition!

Too many people fail before they even start their journey because if you aim too high too soon, you will likely give up because of the amount of time, energy, and effort it takes to see results. So when deciding what to manifest you must be realistic about your current state of being. Get honest with yourself because our current reality is a mirroring of what is going on inside of us.

If you initially aim for something more within your reach, you will quickly see success and thus build the necessary action momentum and confidence to manifest faster and bigger.

#3 Law of Vibration

"Nothing rests, everything moves, everything vibrates."

Everything in the Universe is alive with energy, differing only in rates of vibration. Anything we can see, touch, hear, smell or feel is energy - including you! You - yourself are an energy being.

EVERYTHING IS ENERGY and ENERGY IS EVERYTHING!

As human beings we resonate with our own individual energy that vibrates to a specific pattern of frequencies. We are an aggregate of molecules that make up the genes that make up the DNA that represent your existence.

Albert Einstein's famous equation **$E = mc^2$** states the matter is energy and that energy and mass (and matter) are interchangeable; different forms of the same thing.

Nothing is at rest. Even something that appears to be solid and still, for example a table, is actually in a state of motion as its electrons are alive dancing with energy and movement. Modern science confirms that solidity is indeed an illusion because at the level of atoms and molecules, every particle is vibrating at a certain motion, speed, and frequency. And it is the combination of these factors that determines the physical form of any given object.

Everything is our universe is energy which includes our thoughts. And as our subconscious mind vibrates it attracts the people, events, and circumstances that are at the same vibrational harmony. So be aware of your energetic vibration as that is what has the greatest effect on the quality of your life as you will be undoubtedly attracting matching vibrations to that energy.

#4 Law of Polarity

"Everything is dual; everything has poles; everything has its pair of opposites."

We live in a world of duality. *That means that there is no black without white. No up without down. No left without right. No light without darkness. No pleasure without pain. No success without failure.* There are two sides to everything.

Polarity means that seemingly opposites are not separate at all, they are actually different degrees of the same thing. For example, heat and cold may appear to be opposites but in truth they are just varying degrees of the same thing. The same applies to love and hate, positive and negative, good and evil, energy and matter.

You can either live your dreams or live your fears, you decide!

Everything is on a continuum. This law states that these opposites are simply different manifestations of the same thing! Thus, for every problem, the solution also exists. For every pain, its healing exists. For every desire, its fulfillment exists.

The Universe always seeks balance. And if you can realize that if something negative happens, something positive is available for you. *You just have to seek it out.* If you choose to look for it you then see the opportunities, you then see the people, and the circumstances which will lead you towards your vision that you want to create for your life. It is having an inner knowing that when something bad happens, there is good available.

Fear and depression can be transmuted into love and positivity!

So if you are feeling like you are on the negative spectrum or not where you want to be, know that the opposite is available to you right now.

#5 Law of Rhythm

"Everything flows, out and in; everything has tides; all things rise and fall.... rhythm compensates."

Energy is dynamic, happening in waves and cycles. From the singular molecule to the tides of the ocean, everything is in a state of dynamic change according to the beautiful rhythm of life.

As exemplified by the cyclical changes through the four seasons there is a natural flow we are all part of. Even the economy follows a rhythm as business cycles rise and fall. All things need a period of gestation and growth before reaching maturity. A human baby is born after nine months of being nurtured in the mother's womb. Insomuch, our dream seeds need a period of incubation and growth before we can see them taking form in our physical reality. Be patient as all of our goals need our determination, faith, and strength of will in order to manifest.

The Universe does not make mistakes; you are special and here for a reason! Otherwise you would not be here.

Manifesting your life purpose is divine consciousness manifesting in physical form. The Universe has chosen you to be the shepherd of your unique talents and has presented you with the opportunity to share them for the greater good through your manifestations.

Will you answer the call?

#6 Law of Cause & Effect

"Every cause has its effect; every effect has its cause."

Also known as *karma*, this principle says that there is no such thing as chance. Every thought, every feeling, every action is a cause which has an effect. And it is with these very thoughts, feelings, and actions that shape the world you live in.

You alone are responsible for yourself!

Most people are at the *effect* of the world, not the cause. They are subject to the effect of their thoughts, moods, desires, emotions, and to the whims of other people and the outside environment. However, conscious manifestors have learned how to become the cause and master their own inner reality.

Be the **cause** not the effect.

Being the cause means that you are the master, instead of the being a victim of circumstances. You can become the *cause* of your effect by consciously choosing your reactions, mood, energy, and energetic vibration at all times.

Be proactive – act or be acted upon!

Exercise inspirational and deliberate action, for without proper actions your dreams may whither and atrophy into regrets.

#7 Law of Gender

"Gender is the natural complement to itself."

Gender is in everything. This principle teaches that everything and everyone in the universe possesses both masculine and feminine energy. The creation of thoughts into actions is the result of the masculine and feminine energies working in unison.

As symbolized by the familiar *yin-yang* we must learn to balance and integrate both sides of our being. The feminine and masculine must work together to achieve harmony. One without the other would be imbalanced. It is impossible for creation to take place without this principle.

Masculinity or the left brain embodies yang energy - our *conscious mind.* This is the will, our intellect, our logical/analytic side, it is the source of our desire to achieve something and to take the necessary action.

Femininity or the right brain embodies yin energy - our *subconscious mind.* This is our source of intuition, it is responsible for creativity, feeling, holistic thought, compassion, spontaneity and artistic pursuits.

There is no feminine without masculine. There is no masculine without feminine. We need both.

Now we just succinctly reviewed the Hermetic Principles that governs our material and spiritual life. Knowing the Universal Laws shall open your insights to the deeper spiritual nature of reality. As you begin to understand these laws, you will begin to see them in action everywhere.

By understanding and applying these heavenly principles, you shall become better equipped to control your destiny as you can consciously create your intended reality!

CHAPTER 10

What Are the Top Ways to Reprogram Your Subconscious Mind?

Have you ever wondered why you believe what you believe? Or have you ever thought to think why you think what you think?

Where exactly do our thoughts actually come from?

If you stop and think for a minute you will realize that most of our thoughts, beliefs, and world-views are not original. They are strongly influenced by your culture, families, friends, teachers, the media (TV/movies, music, books), politics, etc. ***They were given to you!***

Ignorance is bliss for most people as they do not know how to think critically while blindly accepting the beliefs that were handed down to them by society. *Until one learns to think for oneself, how can one grow into a more conscious person?* Hack the old draconian system and take the power back by tapping into the power of your own subconscious mind!

Ask yourself: ***Do your current beliefs propel you towards your dreams and goals or do they keep you trapped in mediocrity, monotony, and misery?***

Here are 6 effective methods to reprogramming your subconscious mind:

#1 Set Today's Intentions
Before you do anything, set your intention.

We begin with intention as nothing happens without intent. Your intention can be defined as the ***creative power*** driving your thoughts – it is applied attention. Every move we make or action we take is born from an intention. They are the base foundations of which your goals are created.

Ask and it will be given to you, seek and you will find, knock, and it will be opened to you.
- Matthew 7:7

While goals are focused on your future destinations, intentions should be mindfully aimed at the present moment – on the **RIGHT-HERE-and-NOW**. What you intend with your thoughts is what you will experience in your life - so pay very close attention to your intentions.

Remember, intent is everything!

Once you consciously set your intentions on what you actually want to manifest, you will instantly be more aware of opportunities and attract what you desire seemingly effortlessly.

Exercise: Setting Your Intentions
The intentions you set will direct the decisions you make. Your personal intentions can be declared on any level - physical, financial, social, mental, emotional/spiritual, etc.

By setting your intentions based on your core values and you are creating an alignment with your outer actions and your inner world.

Ask yourself: ***Isn't it time to break the rules of conventional thinking and start thinking for yourself? What are some specific intentions that you want to manifest, right now?***

Here are some sample intentions to inspire you to create your own intentions. The more specific you are, the easier it will be for you to manifest it.

> ***I will live a life of healthy activities, right here and now!***
>
> ***I will watch less television and exercise more, right here and now!***
>
> ***I will devote more energy to my family, friends, and community, right here and now!***
>
> ***I will read more good books, right here and now!***
>
> ***I will volunteer my time for good causes, right here and now!***
>
> ***I will have fun continuously and be open to more every day, right here and now!***

Now, it is your turn:

I will ____ right here and now!

I will ____ right here and now!

I will ____ right here and now!

I will ____ right here and now!

I will ____ right here and now!

I will ____ right here and now!

I will ____ right here and now!

I will ____ right here and now!

I will ____ right here and now!

#2 Start Your Dream Journal

Dreaming is a universal experience - everyone dreams, although not everyone remembers them. *Dream journaling can change all that.*

Consistent dream journaling is another potent tool in the manifestor's arsenal; it is one of the best ways to start remembering your dreams. Your dream journal is an opportunity and space to capture your dreams, find meaning in your dream symbols, and to explore your subconscious mind.

Allow the power of your subconscious mind to achieve your goals while you sleep. Since everything you dream is created by your own mind as you are experiencing it - **dreams are one of the opening gateways to your subconscious mind.** By analyzing your dreamscapes, you can get a more accurate view of yourself and gain navigational insight into your inner world. *Very handy information for your life journey.*

Capturing your dreams on a systematic basis will help align your conscious and subconscious minds. The more often you do this, not only will you start remembering more of your dreams, you will even begin to lucid dream - which is what happens when you realize you are dreaming and ***"wake up"*** while still in your dream.

EXERCISE: Starting Your Dream Journal

Keep a pen handy and first thing upon awakening, write down your dreams in as much vivid detail as possible. Take your time, be patient with yourself - the details will come back to you.

Your dream journal can be a fancy and elaborate leather-bound journal found in a bookstore or it can be as simple as a plain notebook or it could even be any scrap pieces of paper that you can look back to. Online dream journals can work too as long as you can get to your machine quickly as dreams are known to fade quickly.

Answer these questions: ***What was the overall feeling of the dream? What dream symbols were present? Where were you in the dream? Who or what was there with you? What was going on in the dream? What were you and everyone else doing?***

Start your dream journal by answering these headings every day. Write down all you can remember. (Space is also provided in the back of the Playbook to capture all of your dreams.)

LAST NIGHT I DREAMT: ______________________________

Date/Time ______________________________

__________ ______________________________

____

____

____

____

LAST NIGHT I DREAMT: ______________________________

Date/Time ______________________________

__________ ______________________________

____

____

____

____

LAST NIGHT I DREAMT: ______________________________

Date/Time ______________________________

__________ ______________________________

____

____

____

____

#3 Create Your Vision Board

Vision boarding is an extremely simple, fun, and uncannily powerful manifestation tool. A vision board will help you get clear on what you seek and make it indelible in the mind. It makes your goals real and gives them validity. And it helps you get a clear focus on what you really love.

Visualization exercises such as these are known to rewire the brain and connect to the subconscious mind. *Clarify your intentions and clearly visualize what you want.* Leave no doubt. The clearer your intention, the easier it is for you to experience your intentions coming to fruition. Vision boarding can be done on an annual basis such as on New Year's Day or even better, on your birthday.

Where there is no vision the people perish. - Proverbs 29:18

Herein lies the **real secret**. Through the power of creative visualization, you can enable yourself to improve your lifestyle, cause events to happen, and attract people, prosperity, work, possessions, and love into your life simply by their creating their corresponding **mental pictures**. The reason why this works is because the human mind *operates* in pictures.

LIGHTS! CAMERA! ACTION! Visualization is creating a memory of the future right now on the stage of your imagination - *it is about making it happen before it happens.* It is about using the theatre of the mind to see yourself ***being, doing, and having*** all that you desire. **YOU** are the star of the show!

If you can see it in your mind, you can hold it in your hand!

Maybe it is a dream vacation. Maybe it is a new job. Maybe it is a new partner, boyfriend, or girlfriend. Maybe it is a goal to run a marathon. Or maybe your dream is to become an entrepreneur and start your own business. Whatever it may be, a vision board is a fantastic tool to help bring to life what is inside your mind and heart.

It is where fantasy becomes reality!

EXERCISE: Creating Your Vision Board

Go out and find pictures, photos and illustrations of your dreams, goals and aspirations. Choose images that resonate with you and your intentions. This helps make your passions and dreams **tangible.**

Then on a poster board of any type or size, paste or tape those photographs, pictures, inspirational quotes, symbols, words from magazines, and other sources onto the board. You can search online for images and print them out or cut out images from magazines, books or even pictures you draw yourself.

You can even put the images directly onto your bedroom walls. There does not have to be any rhyme or reason of the placement of the images, just get them all up there so you can see them.

So grab a pile of magazines, a pair of scissors, a poster board, and some tape — and get to it!

Now let your subconscious mind get to work for you. *Keep this vision board in a place where you can see it daily.* This could be on your bathroom mirror, on the door or doorway you go in and out of the most, in your bedroom, on your computer, or even in your car. It will help you be focused, motivated, and keep you excited.

#4 Create Positive Power Affirmations

Be alert, for from the moment we wake up into consciousness, everything we do, everything we say, everywhere we go is a decision and an affirmation.

You can train your brain to develop new ways of thinking through the power of affirmations!

An affirmation is any statement of what you desire to create and experience. They keep us in alignment with our intentions and help us replace negative thoughts with positive thoughts.

By using affirmations repeatedly, one can counteract the negative programming of other people, the media, and society has on your perspective on life and it will reprogram your mind for success.

Never underestimate the power of both the written and spoken word!

Both written word and spoken word affirmations are great manifesting tools to start ***materializing*** your intentions. *Every word you think or speak is a thought expressed - it is creative and sends forth creative energy into the Universe.* Thus, by writing down and speaking out loud your intentions continuously, you are now birthing something what was once only in the dimension of your imagination into the dimension of your physical reality. **Words matter.**

Every word is a magic spell. That is why it is called **SPELLING!**

Using affirmations is a psychological technique related to the placebo effect. They are a form of self-induced suggestions or self-hypnosis in which anyone can guide their own thoughts, feelings, and behavior. With practice and if recited consistently with emotion they will directly influence your subconscious mind.

Repetition is key! Repetition is key! Repetition is key!

EXERCISE: Creating Your Power Affirmations

Now it is time to put it in writing. The simplest way to start writing affirmations is to write a series of ***"I AM"*** statements that describe what you want to have or experience. Write down what it is you want to become in the ***PRESENT TENSE*** and verbalize it as if you already fully embodied it.

There is something magical about writing down your intentions for what you add to ***"I AM"*** *- you become*. Choose affirmations that resonate with you and use them as personal mantras. *Speak it into existence - the possibilities are endless!*

For example: **I am capable.**

I am the architect of my life

I am letting happiness manifest in my life.

I am a prosperity and money magnet.

I am actualizing my noblest dreams and highest vision.

I am cool, confident, and accomplish all my objectives.

I am a good leader who knows my purpose.

I am an unlimited being.

I am open to receive.

Now it is your turn to repeat or create your own affirmations and write them down:

I am ____.

I am ____.

I am ____.

I am ____.

I am ____.

I am ____.

I am ____.

I am ____.

You can also begin your affirmations with words such as:

I CAN…... I KNOW…... I HAVE…... I LOVE…...

or any other positive, inspiring, affirmative statement.

Now you have got to ***FEEL IT!*** Write down your affirmations and charge them with passion, emotion, and feeling! ***This is the most important thing!***

Now have them visible where you can see them often, every day.

#5 Practice Daily Meditation

Owning a consistent meditation practice is essential to mastering manifestation and to becoming a conscious creator. Daily meditation is an extremely powerful activity and is a wonderful tool that allows you to reduce stress, deepen awareness of your body, and helps you to enter a calming, dream-like state of being.

One of the best ways to align your conscious and subconscious minds is through meditation. *If your conscious mind and subconscious mind are not aligned, manifestation takes longer.*

Meditating stills your conscious mind, improves cognition, lowers your blood pressure, and helps you focus on your intentions. With the practice of meditation, we will be better able to control our mind, the way we think, the way we feel, and our emotional state.

There is no getting around it — meditation has huge benefits and increases your levels of energy, happiness, inspiration, inner peace, and serenity. Meditation also trains the part of the brain that is responsible for *willpower.*

Meditation can be especially useful when pessimism creeps in. The practice of meditation is quick to learn and does not take much time and the more regularly you are able to practice, the sooner you will experience its transformational power in your life. Through the awareness of the breath, the simple act of noticing the inhale and exhale, we can begin to experience the deeper connection to all things.

EXERCISE: Starting a Daily Meditation Practice

Meditation can be done anywhere at any time. *Just focus on your breath.* It can be done sitting down, lying down, or standing up - *whatever is comfortable for you.*

An easy way to meditate is to go into a quiet area, relax into a comfortable position, and begin to take slow relaxed breaths. Allow your eyes to close and **JUST BREATHE** - take thirty seconds to focus just on your breath. *Breathe in deeply and breathe out slowly.* Doing so helps slow your heartbeat, creates a sense of calm and brings you into the present moment.

Continue to pay attention to your breath, and if you get distracted, return your attention to your breath.

The overall process does not have to take long. Even starting with a 1 or 2-minute silent meditation can have a positive impact on your life. It will also strengthen your mindfulness practice, making it much easier to become present throughout the day. Challenge yourself to meditating for 7 days straight, then 14 days and so on.

#6 Harness the Placebo Effect

Do you want more health, love joy, abundance?

YOU choose!

Placebos are a fanciful way to have a magical effect in your life. The placebo effect is a real phenomenon as it has been replicated time and time again in countless scientific studies and experiments where sick patients receive an innocuous sugar pill with no medicinal value and yet they will begin to heal - merely because they expected that pill to work and help them!

This is definitive evidence of consciousness at work.

Interesting thing about placebos is that they work regardless of you knowing that they are placebos!

Even *knowing* it is a placebo, placebos will still work! Just telling yourself that *"something"* will make something else happen is a very powerful force. What is important is the expectation that something will happen. The placebo effect is concrete proof that through the power of intention and belief people can do incredible things such as heal themselves and others.

EXERCISE: Creating Your Own Placebo Pills

We can create our own placebo pills and get a positive effect from them. Go out and find empty pill capsules and fill them with a harmless substance such as sugar. Then find an empty prescription bottle, peel off the label, and choose what you want the placebo pill to improve for example:

FOCUS

WILLPOWER

HAPPINESS

RELAXATION

INTELLIGENCE

PAIN RELIEF

MORE ENERGY

CONFIDENCE

Now create a new label and add the new label to your bottle. Take your placebo pill every morning or when you feel you need that extra boost.

What kind of "pills" are you going to prescribe yourself today?

CHAPTER 11

What Is the Formula For Manifesting My Dream Life, Right Now?

The best way to understand how manifestation works is to experience it for yourself.

HERE and NOW is your chance!

Step One: IMAGINATION - Visualize Your Ideal Reality

Right now, imagine yourself as your best self - living the life you know that you are worth.

Imagine your highest vibrating self — ***what are you doing?***

Imagine your dream fully realized - sharing that joy, that happiness, that peace with everyone around you.... being the person that you have always known you were destined to become!

What does your dream world, day, job, life.... look like? Let us create the memory of the future event now. ***Where do you see yourself in 3 to 5 years?*** Imagine the sights you will see! Imagine the sounds you will hear! Imagine the scents you will smell! Imagine the feelings you will feel!

What makes you feel most alive? Who will be with you? What view will you have?

Feel the joy and satisfaction of living out your passion! Feel your heart be uplifted with awe and gratitude!

Charge as much emotional feeling into your dreams as you can, emotion is what gives your dreams energy and animation. Think of the raw feelings, exhilaration, and sheer happiness you will feel when you achieve your triumphs! As a result of this sensory enrichment exercise, your subconscious mind will begin to attract what you visualize and make it real. The real-world circumstances to make it living, breathing reality will soon follow.

What could you do? Where could you go? What could you share with the world? What will you manifest? That is right—anything!

EXERCISE: Painting the Big Picture

Now is time to capture what you see playing in the theatre of your mind. On a blank piece of paper, in your journal or in the space below brainstorm and write down all the ideas floating in your head. Once you have all your ideas on paper, you can really start organizing and planning your dreams and goals.

Ask yourself: ***What is your Ultimate Big Life Dream? What would you attempt if you knew you could not fail? If you could manifest ANYTHING in your life right now, what would it be?***

Think carefully about what you want to manifest and write it down in the space provided.

(There are no limits to this brainstorming exercise.)

- -

- -

- -

EXERCISE: Painting the Big Picture - ***What is your Ultimate Big Life Dream?*** (continued)

EXERCISE: Painting the Big Picture - ***What is your Ultimate Big Life Dream?*** (continued)

EXERCISE: Painting the Big Picture - *What is your Ultimate Big Life Dream?* (continued)

Step Two: CLARIFICATION - Clarify Your Top 3 Goals

Your second step is setting the specific goals needed along the way to actualizing your dream. *If you are not absolutely certain about your desires, they will never be fulfilled.*

It is a well-known fact that people who write down their goals and plans are far more likely to accomplish them. Every time you write your goals down on paper, you are gaining clarity around what you desire and plants them squarely into your subconscious - you are literally programming them into your subconscious mind as you would a computer.

And when you program them into your subconscious mind you set up a field of vibration within your brain and throughout your being and based on the Law of Attraction, magnetizes into your life the people, places, and circumstances that harmonize with your dominant thoughts.

Your thought forms need to be crystal clear and explicit if you want to have something tangible materialized. *Clarify how you want to feel as your dreams actualize.* If you do not clearly feel what you want to experience, it will never truly manifest into form for feelings are the real power in manifesting!

Exercise: Describing Your Top 3 Goals

No one can see your vision as clearly as you can. Picture the achievement of each of your top goals happening within the next year. Write down your goals ***AS IF*** you have already achieved them!

Give as much detail as possible and hold this mental picture firmly in your mind's focus. Draw upon all your senses, make the picture as sensory rich as possible: Describe what you see. Describe what you hear. Describe what you feel. Envision as much detail as possible – check out your surroundings: ***Who is with you? What exactly are you doing? Where are you exactly? Now put yourself in the picture!***

Energize all the scenes with emotion!

Imagine it all as being real – RIGHT NOW!

MY TOP 3 GOALS ARE:

(Write your goals in specific, measurable, and time-bound language.)

#1 ____ ________ (due date)

#2 ____ ________ (due date)

#3 ____ ________ (due date)

Step Three: ACTIVATION - Take Deliberate, Inspired Action Daily
Action begins success. Action is the only way to abundance.
This is not a theory – it is a promise!

While most people are waiting for things to happen to them, manifestors make it happen. Too many people nowadays are either so worried about the uncertainties of the future or so caught up dwelling on past mistakes that they totally miss out on the present moment.

Write down your action plans and revise them daily. Action plans are simple prioritized lists of the activities you need to complete a project - they help things get done! These can also serve as daily record.

Your action plan will answer the question: ***What are the tasks required to accomplish each goal?***

A good action plan will help you concentrate your energies, free you from distractions, and boost productivity. Planning your activities will save you time by helping you prioritize what is most important and provides a schedule for the individual steps in the process. Action plans also help determine the resources necessary and what needs to happen to reach your goals. They keep you on track, record what you accomplished, and helps you figure out on what you should work on next.

EXERCISE: Creating Your Action Plan
Make a to-do list of what you need to accomplish to achieve each goal. First ***brainstorm*** every action step you will need to complete your goals. Then prioritize and list all the action steps in the order that you need to complete them. Once that is completed, start with your most important projects of the day and tackle them first.

What action steps will I take today towards my ultimate life dream?

What are the next prioritized actions to reaching my goals?

What do I need to achieve each of my specific goals?

GOAL #1 ACTION STEPS:

(List the specific actions to achieve this goal.)

GOAL #2 ACTION STEPS:

(List the specific actions to achieve this goal.)

GOAL #3 ACTION STEPS:

(List the specific actions to achieve this goal.)

Step Four: NURTURATION - Nurture Your Dream Seeds to Fruition

It is now time to take full and complete ownership of your newly birthed dream for it is a living, breathing entity!

Why is it that some people are successful while other never attain their goals? Anyone can dream it, but you will never see it until you are willing to be committed to it.

Remember, once your dream seeds have been planted, they need to be lovingly nurtured with your energy and attention in order to grow to sweet fruition.

Success journaling accelerates your ability to manifest your goals. Acknowledging your triumphs and victories is a great confidence booster. Record and document your wins. Keeping a journal forces you to commit your goals to writing and when you write down your goals, you are turning vague notions and desires into well-articulated detailed targets you can clearly see and aim for.

Take stock of your day. *Record all the positive moments - big and small.* As you live your best life by implementing your action plan, it is important to keep track of those accomplishments and results. It is always good to look back over and see what went right and what went wrong, and to make course corrections.

Our dreams and goals will often change over time, just as we do. Thus goal-setting is not a one-time activity. Rather, we need to be fluid by continuously reevaluating your dreams and goals, evaluating our progress, and adjusting our actions accordingly.

Keep writing in your Success Journal, do not let that vision board get stale!

Allow yourself to connect with your dream and allow yourself to experience how you will feel when it comes true! Take a few minutes everyday to reflect on your highlights and successes. Nurture it as though it is a living, breathing, and loving thing – ***because it is!***

Our dreams and goals are breathed into being by our conscious thoughts and fueled by our attention and energy. Dreams without action taken upon them will remain as mere fantasies. *Start nurturing your dream seeds today and your heart's desires will manifest beyond your wildest imagination!*

Ask yourself: ***Do you stay connected to your dream and do you nurture it like you would a beloved child?***

Without adequate attention and proper conditions, dream seeds simply cannot manifest properly into physical reality.

If you are not willing to love, nurture, cultivate, and protect your dreams – who will?

Set aside time to evaluate how well your action plan is working. Note what methods worked best to progressing towards your goals. Also note what methods did not work or produce undesired results. It is important not to guess - keep accurate records and examine the numbers. As you constantly read, review, and rewrite your goals, they become *forged into your subconscious mind.*

You can also review your past successes on those days when you feel stuck, discouraged, unfocused, or just need a quick reminder of who you really are. At such times, your Success Journal can reinforce your self-confidence and give you the motivation to move forward in the direction of your dreams.

EXERCISE: Starting Your Daily Success Journal
Start writing down all that you have accomplished this past year. Now is not the time to censor yourself in any way – *your journal is just for you.* Allow yourself to write whatever you feel.

Write with confidence and power. Be specific about what was accomplished, how it made a contribution, and why it is important. Be brave and strengthen your self-confidence systematically by writing in your Success Journal every day.

Ask yourself: ***What progress did I make on my goals today? How did I win the day? Did I learn anything new? Am I making progress? Is there room for improvement? What good did I do today? Which goals of yesterday did I accomplish today? What did I do today to move my goals forward?***

Start by writing at least 3 things that were successful for you today:

1. ____

2. ____

3. ____

CHAPTER 12

What Are the Top Ways to Increase Your Manifesting Potential?

Many people give up on manifestation before any results have been manifested into their lives. They set themselves up to fail by not committing fully or by focusing way, *way too far* ahead into the future.

When you visualize too far ahead in the future, it is difficult to convince your brain. For example, it would be difficult to convince your brain that you are going to be the winning quarterback in the Super Bowl when you have not even played in a high-school football game.

Do not get discouraged if you do these exercises and it appears nothing happens. Manifesting is like a muscle, the more practice, the more natural and powerful it becomes. Exercising your manifesting muscle is like you would your physical muscles at the gym. If you can only lift weights for a few days, you *WILL NOT* see immediate results. But if you keep exercising diligently, your muscles will grow. The same rule applies to exercising your manifesting muscles. Do the exercises on a consistent basis and let the Law of Attraction do the work.

You will be amazed with the results!

The following are the top 21 ways to increase your manifesting potential:

#1 Dream Big, But Start Small

The first part of this simple equation is "dreaming big".

Think acorn and oak tree.

You must dream the biggest dream you can possibly dream. Do not think small just because everyone does. If your dream does not make people uncomfortable or make people think you have gone crazy, that means your dream is not big enough. Your dreams should sound absurd to the average person. So be brave and dream big! DO NOT SET LIMITS ON WHAT YOU CAN DO!

There are endless possibilities when a mind is not influenced by limiting beliefs.

Ask yourself: ***Am I dreaming big enough?***

However, there is a caveat - many rookies to the manifestation game give up too soon because they are too focused on the future and do not start the process at square one.

If you are going to play any game for the first time, you need to practice and learn how to play it. *Put your ego in check.* Start small as small wins compounded over time with patience will add up to something substantial.

So before you think you can win the Super Bowl right away, show that you can win a regular season game. In the same vein, before you manifest your huge mansion with a pool, demonstrate you can handle your current living situation.

If you cannot show that you can take care of what you currently have now, why would the Universe send you more? It will not.

The best advice in manifesting is to start small and build from there. After accomplishing small achievable things then you can move on to greater and greater things. Amazing journeys like that of thousand miles, or your life, are lived one step at a time, one day at a time. It starts with the first step. So remember, dream as big as humanly possible, then take a series of smaller steps to get there.

You are sure to achieve more success with way less stress when you do. A wise person once said that it is where you end up that matters, not where you start.

Practice Self-Love

Manifestation is all about changing yourself into the person you want to be. But before you attempt to change yourself, it is important to accept and love yourself as you are. *If you want to love others, you need to first learn to love yourself.*

How can you truly love someone else until you love yourself and your life? How can you truly help someone be happy, free, peaceful, fulfilled, loving, and blissful until you yourself have those things.

You cannot give what you do not have!

So until you follow your heart, walk your highest path, and stay true to yourself, you are not going to have those things to give others. Additionally, self-love is infinitely important for when you love yourself you are giving others permission to love you.

What can you change or do different to show more loving kindness to yourself?

You deserve to have your heart's desires. The more you love yourself, the faster manifesting happens. So now is the right time to start with yourself!

#2 Keep a Healthy Lifestyle

One of the keys to manifesting quickly is to have high energy levels. And the easiest way to increase those said energy levels is through exercise, proper rest, and consuming a natural, balanced, nutritious diet.

It is with your earthly body that you experience and navigate through this waking life, by keeping it as healthy as possible you will not have to waste your energy dealing with the complications of physical dis-ease, and instead you will be able to focus on your visions. Because until you get your health in order, you will never reach your full potential.

Your body is a reflection of your mind and what you think in your mind will manifest in your body. Your diet is not just what you eat. It is what you watch. It is what you read. It is who you are around and what you absorb from your environment.

It is no secret that exercise is an essential part of a healthy, balanced and productive lifestyle. Consistent exercise is one of the largest known contributors to increasing natural energy levels, elevating metabolism, enhancing the immune system, improving mood, sleep and lowering overall stress and anxiety. Also, a healthy nutrition plan is essential for optimum brain health and concentration. Eating too much will slow you down and can lead to feeling tired and sluggish, while eating too little can lead to hunger distraction.

Because there are so many benefits of a fitness lifestyle that starting any exercise program is highly recommended - even if it is only a few minutes a day. *Be proactive about your health.* You can start by simply walking and increase the amount and variety of exercises as you go. Choose fun and meaningful activities so that you will look forward to exercising and it becomes its own reward.

Optimal performance is also not possible without proper rest and relaxation so make sure you get enough sleep and take those vacation days. By working on your body, you are preparing your mind.

Plenty of people often say they will do better tomorrow. But then it comes to your health, doing better needs to start today. **Health is true wealth.** Go out and exercise! Be active! Move your body!

Excuses or results, you choose.

#3 Get Outdoors

Have you ever noticed that going outside and reconnecting with nature makes you happier with less stress? Whether it is a walk on a sandy beach, a swim in the ocean, a long bike-ride, a hike in a green forest, or a trek up a rugged mountain - there is something enchanting about being immersed in nature. Just the scent of flowers alone can heal your soul, make you happy and dissipate negativity!

Regrettably however, in today's modern society people are spending less and less time outdoors and significantly more time disconnected from nature, indoors in artificial, temperature-controlled environments causing stress and anxiety.

Scientific research has proven again and again the healing power of spending time in natural settings. Intuitively people know that spending time outdoors is good for you. It can help you feel calmer, happier, more focused, less stressed and at peace with yourself and others. Nature has its own way of healing.

From now on, be sure to spend as much time as you can in the company of nature and reap the benefits of it. Take a day, or a weekend, to live your life without the internet and other modern distractions. Be inspired to go out and rediscover the wonders of the natural world!

So go play outside. Spend time with your loved ones. Enjoy the sunset, go stargazing. Be like a child again. Be in the elements. Take a trip. Take the long way home.

They do not call it the ***"Great Outdoors"*** for nothing!

#4 Start Giving Back

True success begins the very moment we begin giving back.

The act of giving shifts your perspective as nothing makes your personal problems seem insignificant like helping those less fortunate. Giving back is like gratitude - it makes us feel good inside. When you choose to give selflessly without expecting anything in return, you are now part of something larger than yourself.

Most people are waiting to get something before they will give - *do not be like most people.* Never do our hearts feel fuller than when are selflessly offering ourselves to those in need of support. You can bask in the joy that giving brings to those you have helped. Imagine how ecstatic you will feel once you give!

Give what it is you seek. Give help if you want help, give love if you want love, give praise if you want praise, give money if you want money, or teach someone something that you would like to learn yourself.

Giving is ***the secret*** to receiving. Giving begins the receiving cycle. Another not-so-secret to life is to give what you want to receive. Giving and receiving is a cycle that is one whole and the act of giving actually starts the receiving cycle.

Giving is the only way to receive more. Also allow yourself to receive as it allows others their opportunity to give.

There are countless way to get involved with volunteering, philanthropy, and giving back. Start with your own family and your own community and branch out from there. It does not have to be about money, you can give your time, you can give your warmth and friendship. It could be a smile on the street to a stranger, it could be a day of volunteering, or it could be helping an elder put their groceries in their vehicle.

Sometimes the smallest things can make the biggest difference!

According to the Universal Laws, when you give it may not come back to you from where you expect it, but it always does. All of the energy and intentions you put out there will always recirculate and finds its way back to you.

When you hold back out of fear, you are reinforcing lack and scarcity thus blocking yourself from the natural flow of life.

Go out and donate and see how it feels. It should feel great. Use that feeling to spur you on to further acts of kindness in the future. Take the lead, it is time to make an impact and make a real lasting difference in this world.

#5 Get Out of Your Comfort Zone

Great lives are not made in comfort.

Although routine and familiarity may feel comforting, it is a nefarious and hidden trap. When you are in your comfort zone and all your needs are met and you have zero stress, your brain does not want anything to change. But when the human mind is challenged, it responds in remarkable ways and the further it is pushed, the more wondrous the responses will be. For those of you seeking to become the best version of yourself, your ability to embrace the uncertainty that comes with stepping out of your comfort zone is necessary for success.

When was the last time you stepped out of your comfort zone?

The average person wants to play it safe and have a safe job and a have a comfortable life and live within the lines. If you are ok with living in your comfort zone for the rest of your days, there is nothing inherently wrong with that. You can join the majority of people who plan their lives around the pursuit of comfort and end up living lives of boredom, unhappiness, meaninglessness, misdirection, and depression.

But the reality is that greatness often takes the appearance of discomfort and those who are willing to take risks and step out of their comfort zone are those who will reap the biggest rewards.

No risk, no reward.

It takes guts to act, to accept a risk and do something new. ***Discomfort is your friend.*** To make progress, you need to feel a little pressure. Take risks - life is an inherently risky undertaking. In fact, none of us are going to get out of this alive. So why not go for it and live the life you desire? Do not be afraid of experimenting with new ideas as it is known that growth can only occurs during times of discomfort.

Once you are outside your comfort zone you may find it easy to give into worry or doubt. It can be a scary place if you are new to stepping out of the comfort zones set up by society. Now is a time to trust yourself and the process.

Greatness is on the other side of pain!

Change begets change. So do something different for a change. The comfortable road will never lead you to the person you were destined to be!

Step away from complacency and take action. No matter how small, take the first step. There are lots of other ways to stretch your personal boundaries. Step out of your comfort zone and try new things - often. Open new doors and you will gain new profound experiences.

#6 Get Into A Powerful Peak State

Have you ever felt like you were "in the zone"? Or have you ever had times in your life where you felt just so alive, unstoppable, and excited - where ideas and energy was just flowing through you and everything was just falling into place? You, my friend was operating from a "Peak State" where you feel like you are invincible and can accomplish anything!

Peak state is when you perform at your best. It is when you have the confidence that it is all possible - no matter what the obstacles may appear to be. Emotions propel your manifesting message. Your ***heart***, not your mind is your most powerful tool in manifesting.

Goals are more easily achieved when you are in a high vibrational state of emotion! So get yourself into a peak state in the morning and you can operate from that state for the rest of your day.

Feeling is the force of attraction. Once you have that feeling of success, do whatever it takes to stay in that potent emotional state as often as possible as you vividly imagine what it will be like once your goal manifests. The more time you spend in that emotional state or "***vibration***", the sooner your goal will appear.

Getting into a peak state is easy! Anything that will give you inspiration and energy will work. Go ahead and rewind and relive your past triumphs and achievements in the theatre of the mind. Picture the time when you achieved something you set out to do. Think back through the past to a time you felt totally confident and in control of what was taking place. Or think about an inspiring or exciting event in the future.

Get active! Move your body! Take a deep breath! Breathing deeply is one the easiest ways to transform into a peak state!

Listening to motivational music or your favorite track can also easily trigger a peak state. Music can move people in ways that nothing else can. *Music has the ability to spark the flame of any emotion!* Or watch a scene from a movie that pumps you up. Learning and expanding your mind can put you into a peak state. Or by spending time with those who inspire you and uplift you can completely change your energy. Giving to others and being kind to someone can also put you into a super-charged, incredible mood.

Remember those feelings? Now hold on to those feelings! Practice until you can summon these feelings on demand.

#7 Align Yourself with Powerful People

Success breeds success.

Take a good look at the people around you. You are who you surround yourself with. Building a network of like-minded friends and mentors is one of the most beneficial things you can do as a manifestor. It is a great way to increase your manifesting potential exponentially.

Community is important. Choose the people you surround yourself with wisely….and that can make all the difference in your life - for who you spend time with is who you become. Relationships are either nourishing or toxic. Take the time to be brutally honest with yourself and your relationships.

Ask yourself: ***Does being with this person energize me or deplete me?***

It has been said that you are the average sum of the 5 people you surround yourself the most, so align yourself with positive-minded people who uplift you, encourage you, and support you. Seek people you can learn from, people you can grow from.

It is time to weed the garden and provide a platform for maximum personal growth! Get rid of parasites and energy drainers! Eliminate or at least minimize the negative people in your life as they can impede your progress. Avoid those who are stuck in unhealthy habits, who always play the victim, or anyone that generally makes you feel drained or bad about yourself.

Take steps to end any toxic relationships and invite more positive people into your inner circle and life. Ask yourself if each person is nourishing you or acting as a toxic agent. If they are not on the side of what good is for you, walk away. Instead, surround yourself with those who are positive, productive, focused, and ambitious - ***the same path that you are on!***

#8 Turn Off Negativity

A negative mind will never give you a positive life.

The eradication of negative self-talk as your inner dialogue is a key component in developing a true manifestor's mindset. *Pay attention to your self-talk!* For if you plant your dream seeds in a heart and mind that is infected with doubts and polluted with negativity, they will not thrive properly.

By engaging in negative self-talk consistently, you start to believe it which erodes your self-image. In order to consciously break the recycling of negative and debilitating psychological patterns, keep your heart centered on what you love. Decide right now to turn off the negative news channel that runs constantly in many people's heads.

Create such a wave of positivity that it drowns out any negativity!

It is also very important to understand that whenever you start the journey of manifesting your dreams, you may come across many negative beliefs and people. There will always be people who try to discourage you. There will be naysayers and *"Negative Nancie's"* and *"Debbie Downers"* who have not achieved their own goals who will try to discourage you from achieving yours.

Do not let anyone - friend, family member, teacher, acquaintance or anyone tell you that it is not possible - *IT IS POSSIBLE!*

Therefore, make sure to choose your friends carefully. Do not let their negative beliefs and small-minded fears act as barriers to making your dreams come true. Do not listen to them. I repeat, **do not listen to them**. Pay them no mind as the only limit is the one you set for yourself. Instead spend time with friends who have uplifting spirits and positive mindsets, they will help you to grow into the best version of yourself.

Eliminate negative words and phrases such as *"CAN'T"*, *"TRY"*, and *"I SHOULD"*. To most people, these words are a harmless part of everyday speech, but to the conscious manifestor, words spoken create reality.

Saying *"I can't"* is one of the most negative affirmations out there. This is the first phrase that needs to be completely wiped from your working vocabulary. *It is not even a real word.* Just by uttering these words, you are totally shutting down your vibration and hampering your ability to accomplish anything. Never say these words again. The only limit is the one you put on yourself.

Saying *"I will try"* is also another way to set yourself up for failure. There is a built-in excuse for failure when you say, "I will try". Commit one way or the other. It is either "I will" or "I won't".

"Try" is a useless word. Either put 100% into it or do not do it at all. There is a big difference between *doing* and *trying.*

Saying *"I should"* do or be something is based on the expectations of others. It is rooted in guilt, pressure and negativity - "should" is a pointless word. "Should" is focused on what is lacking. When used we are reinforcing the negative and the fact that we are not doing it. Avoid passing unnecessary judgment on yourself or the situation. It is all just empty talk - lip service. Replace "I should" with "I will."

Take notice every time you hear yourself or someone else around you use these words and phrases. Before speaking, make it a habit to choose your words carefully. Be diplomatic towards yourself and others. By creating awareness, you will begin to notice how often it actually pops up in your thoughts and speech. Awareness is the first step to changing a habit.

Now that you are aware of these disempowering words, removing and replacing these words with more helpful dialogue will lead to a more empowering relationship with yourself and with the people around you too. Positively reframe your sentences and you will be able to command your subconscious mind to find ways of achieving your goals instead of losing the game before it even gets started.

Seek out using positive words that encourage and build up others and motivate them to do better. You will find greater satisfaction, happiness, and success in all your relationships instantly.

#9 Cultivate Optimism

They say beauty is in the eye of the beholder, but equally so are love, truth, happiness, and optimism. *There is nothing you cannot be, do, or have!* It is your perception holds the key to your reality.

Optimism is defined as having a positive mental attitude reflecting a confidence about the future. Do not let circumstances dictate your success. *There will always be obstacles to be overcome!*

One of the best gifts you can give yourself is a positive attitude. Having this positive frame of mind will not only increase your physical and mental health and lower your stress level, it will shift your entire perspective on life.

Unnecessary worry will stunt the growth of your dreams!

Today, change the way you think. Believing in yourself is a choice. The past does not have to determine your present anymore. When you choose to start focusing on the brighter side of things, our life becomes an infinite field of new possibilities. *For the optimist the glass is always half full!* Through the power of positive thinking, you can overcome any obstacle and make each of your dreams come true.

You can accomplish anything you set your mind to. This has been proven time and time again. Replacing negative thoughts and words with optimistic ones brings oh so many benefits. When fostering an optimistic outlook, you will be more resilient, and it will also make you look and feel better – from the inside-out.

You can do much more than you think!

So free yourself from the restraints of old negative habits, self-doubt and self-criticism. Stop being afraid of what could be wrong - instead start thinking unlimited and focus on what could go right. Once you do this, you may feel a lightness of being, renewed confidence, and experience spontaneous joyfulness!

#10 Learn to Adapt

Change is the only constant, so learning to adapt to new situations and people is paramount to thriving in this ever-changing world. So please do not be so unbending in the application of the Universal Laws for taking the manifestation process too seriously makes it much harder for us to be aware of our reality.

Life is always changing. Be flexible and stay fluid.

Embracing flexibility can help you deal with all kinds of life situations. The only sure thing about life is that nothing stays the same. Learn to adapt with changes, not fight against them for the more easily you can adapt to new situations, the more successful and happier you will be.

Old thinking cannot solve new problems; so your ability to adapt can create major changes in your health, wealth, and personal relationships. Open up your heart and mind to new adventures and concentrate on how you can grow and develop yourself during these new challenges. It is about finding comfort in being uncomfortable and growing with the flow - *embracing this is the key to happiness.*

The feeling of uncertainty and unease with a new situation is totally normal and to be overcome. Do not be so quick to place judgement on a new position or set of circumstances.

You could be missing out on a great once-in-a-lifetime experience!

#11 Cut Out Distractions

How many times per day are you being distracted? We are all given the same 24 hours in a day to use in the best way we see fit. *How you use that given time determines your destiny.*

The greatest minds in history know how to *tune out the noise. Tune out the critics. Tune out the doubters. Tune out the haters.*

If you want to really focus on your manifestations, it is of utmost importance that you cut out as many distractions as you can. Those that master the art of self-control are often found at the top of their respective industries.

In a world full of incessant distractions, it is small wonder that those who achieve the greatest triumphs in life have learned to manage them effectively. Entertaining distractions not only robs you of your time, your most precious resource, but also comes with an opportunity-cost as you could be focusing on your own manifestations.

We can be so absorbed by the meaningless distractions of life that we become blinded to the magnificent blessings around us. Thus, we need to wake up and appreciate and enjoy our blessings - *here and now* - while we have them!

For example, do not waste your life on your mobile phone. Learn to leverage the technology, while preventing it from derailing your success. It is important to remove these distractions, so we do not lose our connection to our dreams and goals. When you master this self-control skill, there is nothing else to stand in your way of greatness!

So be mindful and take a cold hard look at how you spend your precious time.

#12 Turn Off the Television

Watching TV is a big-time time-waster!

In our modern-day society, television is a major part of our everyday lives, with the average person expending five or more hours a day watching television, also known as the "idiot-box"! *Most are completely unaware of how negatively it is influencing them.*

Television is a tremendously powerful medium. It is one of the greatest and most effective devices of mass mind control ever invented. Watching television and movies is a passive activity where your mind enters a state of high suggestibility. While it may be argued that watching educational and other positive minded programs helps increase one's knowledge quotient, the risks far outweigh the benefits.

Most people just accept the "TV Reality" they have been presented as real-life. They live in a world of "make believe" and "fake news" where the media decides what is true and false and what is up and down. By turning on the "boob tube", you are allowing the corporations and advertisers to stream their products, ideas, and agendas directly into your subconscious mind. For hours on end you literally just hand over your consciousness to the machine. They know that the subconscious mind absorbs at a rapid rate like a sponge and most people blindly accept whatsoever television is feeding them both consciously and subconsciously.

Did you know that sitting in front of the TV and inactivity has been linked to obesity and heart disease? So not only does prolonged viewing hurt your health and reduce your quality of life, it impedes you from your own manifestation activities!

Watching TV is one of today's biggest and most effective distractions. Instead of living our life to the fullest, we have chosen entertainment as a substitute for true living. Are you one of those addicted to watching the evening news or other "fear porn"? *Turn off anything that constantly reminds you to fear and lower your vibrations.*

Television is a steady stream of with lies, deception, fear, misinformation, and confusion. It deceives you by making you focus all of your attention on superficial matters and neglect what is truly important in life.

They do not call it "programming" for nothing!

Believe it or not, your subconscious mind is always on and recording everything. So whoever controls your subconscious mind controls the world you create. Put an end to regular television watching and you will start spending your time much more creatively and productively and discover more joy, mental clarity, and peace of mind. You will be amazed how turning off the TV can have a major impact on your state of mind.

Use your time wisely. Turn it off, even better - throw it away!

#13 Carry a Symbol or Talisman

Ever have a lucky rabbit's foot, 4-leaf clover, special amulet, or other good luck charm when you were a child?

Talismans are physical objects used for the bearing of a charged intent. Carrying these objects with you serve as a reminder and constant way to anchor yourself to your belief that you can attract what you desire. *Symbols and talismans have the power to represent your desires and remind you what is important.*

Choose an object that represents your Big Dream or other intention. It can be anything of your choice. It can be any object, perhaps a photograph, a rock, gemstone or crystal, piece of jewelry, or anything you can carry with you that prompts you to focus on your specific intention. *You determine what the talisman's purpose is.* Let the object become the physical representation of an intention, desire, or positive emotion (i.e. luck, health, love, abundance, etc.).

It will act as a trigger to shift negative thoughts to positive affirmations that support you in your manifesting goals. For example, your chosen object will elevate your consciousness as it reminds you of the feeling and state of abundance. Keep your talisman nearby where you can see it regularly and use it. Your symbol or talisman can serve to remind you of something important or can be used in stressful situations, as well as when you need more luck.

Take a few moments to meditate or pray using your chosen symbol or talisman to charge it up with positive energy as needed.

#14 Blur the Line Between Work and Play

The manifestation process is all about living life to the fullest, so above all, have fun with it!
Let it be joyous!

When we are passionate about what we do, we are more likely to develop a focus that yields the best results. When we love what we do, *we do it better.* It is true when they say that if you do what you love, then you will never have to work another day in your life.

What is your passion in life?

A balance needs to be maintained between work and play. It is during play that you recreate your mind. Blur the line between work and play as much as possible as your best work is done doing that which you enjoy most.

Whether at work, school, or home, find ways to integrate playfulness and curiosity to help fuel our creativity, motivation, and commitment to whatever it is that you are engaging in. Play is an important as work so if you are not having fun, then you are not doing it right. The more fun you have, the more likely it is that you are vibrating at a frequency to attract your dreams to you.

You need to bring fun into the whole creation process - a playful seriousness. Work without play becomes mundane, tedious, and non-fulfilling. *So if you are not having some fun along the way, you are doing something wrong, terribly wrong!*

Playfulness and lightheartedness, when joined with the knowledge of the manifestation process, make the ideal formula for manifesting your dreams!

Let your unique process unfold naturally – forcing it will not work in the long-term.

#15 Avoid Materialism

Look around you today. It is no secret that we are living in a materialistic-based society with a consumer culture where the majority of people are trapped in the fog and endless cycle of materialism.

These simple-minded folks are very materialistic, superficial, and short-sighted in the life goals they set for themselves. They mistakenly believe that consuming more and more material things and acquiring more and more material objects is the main purpose of human existence. This false, overly materialistic sense of identity is the source of these people's unhappiness and general dissatisfaction with life.

Now avoiding materialism is not about forsaking the material world or giving away all your possessions. There is nothing inherently wrong with owning material objects or living in luxurious settings. *The problem is not the material objects themselves.* The issue arises when there is excessive emphasis on these material items combined with the neglect of higher spiritual values.

Real prosperity and true wealth are not based on material possessions!

Another problem with focusing too much on material goods is that it will never be enough. Material objects can only afford us a temporary fleeting gratification for our minds become quickly conditioned to what we have. *True wealth comes from within.*

Advertisers and corporations have brainwashed people to believe that objects and a flashy lifestyle are the true representations for happiness and success. No wonder the masses of people mistake the symbols of success and wealth for success itself. Conscious manifestors realize that material rewards and possessions such as mansions, fast cars, expensive watches, extravagant jewelry, and fancy wardrobes are the **byproducts** of success - ***not success itself!***

Wake up!

Take a reprieve from commercialism. Stop getting dragged down by society's expectations and delusions. You do not have to keep up with the Jones. You do no need *this or that* to fulfill you!

Being materialistic distracts us from the important things that really matter in life such as self-growth, being compassionate and helping others, and building meaningful lasting relationships.

As modern society delegates people into weak-willed mindless consumers, please remember we are spiritual beings having a human experience, thank you!

#16 Trust Your Gut

Ever have a gut feeling about something?
Well, your gut is your second brain.

Did you know that there are more nerve endings in your gut than in your brain? Some call it our sixth sense or intuition, whatever you call it we all possess the capacity to feel and know things without conscious reasoning. It is beyond the rational, reasoning mind to comprehend.

Your intuition is your connection to the divine.

We all have the gentle inner voice of intuition and listening to this voice is to open ourselves up to the deep wisdom contained within.

Start to listen to yourself more, trust yourself more, and know that that quiet little voice inside knows what is best for you. You know you better than anyone. So if something just does not feel right, listen to your body, and act accordingly.

Take time to listen to your inner voice - that is your gut, your intuition and it is never wrong!

Our intuition is the communication channel between our conscious and subconscious minds. And no matter what form manifestation takes, intuition is at its base. It functions as our internal compass guiding us and giving us a "feeling" about what to do in certain situations.

Focus on trusting and listening to your intuition. Take a pause and let the "ah-ha moments" guide you. Notice opportunities that keep presenting themselves to you. Pay attention to what your body is telling you. Drown out the external voices telling you what to do and what not to do. *Instead replace those voices with your own.*

The more we understand and develop from *within* the more harmonious and balanced our lives will become.

#17 Embrace Synchronicity

Nothing is a coincidence.

Everything that is meant to happen will happen.

Synchronicity is defined as the simultaneous occurrence of events which apparently have no clear cause, but in actuality are deeply meaningful. Although life at times seems random and ruled by meaningless happenstance, life is really an intricate web of interconnectedness. There is a message for you there. Synchronicity is about realizing the meaningful coincidences in the seemingly mundane.

Synchronicities come our way as we are in harmony with the Universe. Every single coincidence is bringing a message to you. There are no accidents; there are only synchronicities as everything happens for a reason.

It is divine confirmation that you are on the right track!

There are countless ways synchronicity shows up in your life. Ever see someone doing the same thing or speaking the same words as you? Or you could be thinking about something and it suddenly appears as if on cue. Or you could be thinking about someone and suddenly they appear out of seemingly nowhere. Or have you ever met someone out of the blue who appears to answer your inner questions?

These meaningful moments are evidence belying the hidden order of things revealing an underlying pattern that organizes all of our lives. What most people think are just random coincidences, conscious manifestors recognize as *synchronicity.*

It also happens through numbers. Do you ever notice the same numbers or repeating numbers keep showing up in your life over and over? Of course, the list of synchronicities can be endless. Pay attention to these synchronistic events as they have guidance for you. Synchronistic moments are signs to show you that you are in proper alignment with the path that you are supposed to be on. *It is a sure sign life is in flow!*

The more you raise your vibration, the more synchronistic experiences you will have. If you are in a state of negative emotions and thus oscillating at lower vibrations, you will not have as much as you are not fully able to be aware of the magnificence around you.

#18 Avoid Perfectionism

Nobody's perfect.

So if you are expecting perfection or needlessly clinging onto unrealistic ideals, you will always be disappointed.

Perfectionism has been the reason for many people to stop before they even begin. Now the relentless pursuit of excellence is a wonderful and noble aspiration, but when it spills over into perfectionism it can be just as debilitating as incompetence. *It is okay to allow yourself to fail, as failure is a much better teacher than success!*

Do not get trapped into a "paralysis by analysis" situation by overthinking. Perfectionists often hinder their own success by being too attached to unrealistic ideals. They focus too much on the results instead of the process. And they are always afraid of being judged. Embrace imperfection, make mistakes - it is all part of the learning process that has to happen.

Give yourself the same permission that you give others to make mistakes. Do this for yourself today.

You deserve it!

#19 Be a Lifelong Learner

Life is a school. If you are still alive then that means you still have something yet to learn.
So never be content with only what you know now.

Manifestors are continuously improving their game in all spheres of life. Make a conscious commitment to learn new ways to continue your education, expand your mind, and to improve your personal and professional skills. Embrace the beginner's mindset - the idea is to approach every person, experience, and action as if it is for the first time with no prejudices.

Become a lifelong learner.... So **you** – not your parents, not your professors, not your boss — get to decide what you are going to learn about. Instead of being just a passive consumer of institutionalized knowledge, you are now actively choosing what you are learning. Not only does lifelong learning help you earn more in traditional employment, lifelong learning is the gateway to self-reliance, self-employment, and starting your own business.

What is something new you can learn about today?

Go ahead and challenge yourself today. The entire world is your classroom. There is always more to learn.

#20 Celebrate Your Success

Do not forget to celebrate along the way, for celebration is a sign of maturity and another secret key to manifestation!

Recognizing and validating the great things you do is more important than you can imagine. One of the best reasons to celebrate success is simply that it feels good. And feeling good is what it is all about after all, isn't it?

What accomplishments can you celebrate today?

When you take the time to celebrate progress and to applaud our achievements, you are acknowledging all the work that is getting done and will inspire even greater achievements. Neglecting to celebrate your successes along the way can cause physical and mental burn-out. And you may subconsciously begin to take a negative view on your accomplishments.

A proper celebration can boost your confidence, help to stave off burn-out, and fuel your continued success. So, take a moment to celebrate your success and honor you. Find one thing to celebrate every day.

#21 Let Go

Life is an exhilarating and often mysterious trip and the ultimate secret is in *letting go.*

That does not mean to give up or stop caring - it means to relax, show some faith, and understand that control is yet another illusion. It is about allowing things to happen in your life easily and naturally. *Let go the burden of all those expectations!*

The ultimate goal of the manifestor is not to succeed or fail, the ultimate goal is to give everything you have for something that is in your heart.

After imagining the **WHAT**, leave the ***HOW*** open. Once you are clear about what you want, you have done your part. After that you cannot control the timing or the form in which it comes. The **HOW** will take care of itself. *You just have to be open to what comes.*

So let go of any judgements about how the details should manifest or come to you. Allow things to happen organically. The people, new ideas, technology, and circumstances will appear to help you achieve your dreams at the right time.

Your part is to generate clear goals, believe in them passionately, take practical action to move towards them, keep the faith, and let the Universe do its part.

By detaching from the outcome, you are relinquishing your attachment to a specific result and instead choosing to live in the wisdom of the moment. *As you release your emotional attachments, negative thoughts, worry, and tension will leave your body.*

When you trust in the Universe you will find true abundance, joy, health, love, success and prosperity. As you let go of negativity and disbelief, you will be guided to the right events to bring your dreams to life. All you have to do is believe that your dreams are possible and that they are coming towards you now!

What are you needlessly holding onto?

Letting go will allow your deepest desires to begin manifesting. It is about getting out of your own way and allowing the Law of Attraction to bring you your desires. Surrender and prepare to be amazed beyond belief! Remember, worry is a prayer for what you do not want. The more you worry about them, the more problems you attract.

Just Let Go!

CONCLUSION

Real Magic!

As you can see, "manifestation" is not something supernatural, miraculous or *"out of this world."* Manifestation is simply aligning yourself with your intentions/goals then taking the necessary steps to bring those intentions/goals to fruition.

Here, now the real work begins. I have merely shown you the door. Through the power of the mind you have the ability to create, control, and shape reality. *This is the real magic of life!* Now it is ***solely up to you*** to take the first step towards to living your dream.

The knowledge in this book is a good starting point but if you want radical success it is going to be your conscious actions from this moment forward that will determine your future. I urge you to do the exercises laid out for you – they are in this guide for a reason. Not just theory or guesswork - instead, what you are about to discover first-hand has been proven in the field countless times. *It works if you work it.* Open your heart and mind then apply these concepts and results will follow - *we guarantee it!*

Whether your dreams come true right away in an instant or they take a while, whether the path is exceptionally bumpy or oddly super smooth - as long as your heart continues working towards those dreams, you should know they will come true.

You can absolutely do it!

Your entire life is based on the choices you make - whether consciously or unconsciously - there is a consequence. Release your old fears and the little voice in your head that says to make limited choices based on past experiences. *It is okay to be great.* Give yourself permission to be the greatest **YOU** that you can be! Be confident, step into your power. The greatest positive changes in our lives come when we throw caution to the wind and just go for it!

Then soon, one day according to your vibration, you will wake up living the dream you created – *that dream that was once just a thought in your mind.* You will be able to bear witness to the real results that the magic of manifestation can do!

BE THE MASTER MANIFESTOR THAT YOU ARE!

The door has been opened now. It is up to ***YOU*** to walk through it. However you begin.... begin! *It is a life changing choice.* Go and consciously create. Do not wait or procrastinate - start today.

Do It Now!

SPACE TO DREAM

SPACE TO DREAM

SPACE TO DREAM

SPACE TO DREAM

SPACE TO DREAM

SPACE TO DREAM

SPACE TO DREAM

SPACE TO DREAM

SPACE TO DREAM

SPACE TO DREAM

SPACE TO DREAM

SPACE TO DREAM

SPACE TO DREAM

SPACE TO DREAM

SPACE TO DREAM

SPACE TO DREAM

SPACE TO DREAM

SPACE TO DREAM

SPACE TO DREAM

SPACE TO DREAM

SPACE TO DREAM

ABOUT THE AUTHOR

Steve L Chong is an author, speaker, activist, multimedia artist, serial entrepreneur, international traveler, philanthropist, photographer, marketing consultant and business mentor. He is also the author of *The Entrepreneur's Playbook: How to Startup Your Dream Business.*

Steve leads workshops, retreats and seminars throughout the world focusing on entrepreneurship, prosperity, abundance, and spirituality, and his articles have been published in a multitude of magazines, journals, and websites across the United States and internationally. He has been a featured, sought-after speaker at numerous yoga festivals and business conferences helping attendees actualize their dreams.

A graduate of the University of Illinois-Urbana Champaign, where he received a Bachelor of Arts in Liberal Arts. Steve lives in Chicago, IL, when not on the road living in his RV.

And his personal one-on-one coaching sessions are available throughout the year, either in person, online or on the phone.

Made in the USA
Las Vegas, NV
11 February 2022